WORKBOOK

Cambridge IGCSE™ and O Level

Business

Third Edition

Karen Borrington
Peter Stimpson

Introduction

Welcome to the Cambridge IGCSE™ and O Level Business Workbook. The aim of this Workbook is to provide you with further opportunity to practise the skills you have acquired through using the Cambridge IGCSE and O Level Business Student Book. It is designed to complement the 6th edition of the Student Book and to provide additional exercises to help you practise your skills and prepare for assessment. This Workbook covers the content of the Cambridge IGCSE and O Level syllabuses.

The chapters in this Workbook reflect the topics in the Student Book. There is no set way to approach using this Workbook. You may wish to use it to supplement your understanding of the different topics as you work through each chapter of the textbook, or you may prefer to use it to reinforce your skills in dealing with particular topics as you revise. The Workbook is intended to be sufficiently flexible to suit whatever you feel is the best approach for your needs. Answer lines have been provided but do not necessarily indicate length of response. You may need additional paper for some questions, particularly those with a higher mark allocation.

This text has not been through the endorsement process for the Cambridge Pathway. Any references or materials related to answers, grades, papers or examinations are based on the opinion of the author(s). The Cambridge International Education syllabus or curriculum framework associated assessment guidance material and specimen papers should always be referred to for definitive guidance.

All questions have been written by the authors.

Every effort has been made to trace all copyright holders, but if any have been inadvertently overlooked the publishers will be pleased to make the necessary arrangements at the first opportunity.

Although every effort has been made to ensure that website addresses are correct at time of going to press, Hachette Learning cannot be held responsible for the content of any website mentioned in this book. It is sometimes possible to find a relocated web page by typing in the address of the home page for a website in the URL window of your browser.

Hachette UK's policy is to use papers that are natural, renewable and recyclable products and made from wood grown in well-managed forests and other controlled sources. The logging and manufacturing processes are expected to conform to the environmental regulations of the country of origin.

To order, please visit www.hachettelearning.com or contact Customer Service at education@hachette.co.uk / +44 (0)1235 827827.

ISBN: 978 1 0360 1072 0

© Karen Borrington and Peter Stimpson 2025
Hachette Learning,
An Hachette UK Company
Carmelite House
50 Victoria Embankment
London EC4Y 0DZ

www.hachettelearning.com

The authorised representative in the EEA is Hachette Ireland, 8 Castlecourt Centre, Dublin 15, D15 XTP3, Ireland (email: info@hbgi.ie)

Impression number   10 9 8 7 6 5 4

Year   2028 2027 2026

All rights reserved. Apart from any use permitted under UK copyright law, no part of this publication may be reproduced or transmitted in any form or by any means, electronic or mechanical, including photocopying and recording, or held within any information storage and retrieval system, without permission in writing from the publisher or under licence from the Copyright Licensing Agency Limited. Further details of such licences (for reprographic reproduction) may be obtained from the Copyright Licensing Agency Limited, www.cla.co.uk

Cover photo © Sergey Nivens - stock.adobe.com
Illustrations by Aptara Inc.
Typeset in India by Aptara Inc.
Printed in the UK by Bell & Bain Limited

A catalogue record for this title is available from the British Library.

Contents

SECTION 1 Understanding business activity
1. Business activity and economic sectors — 4
2. Enterprise, business growth and size — 6
3. Types of business organisations — 9
4. Business objectives and stakeholder objectives — 12
   Case study — 15

SECTION 2 People in business
5. Human resource management (HRM) — 17
6. Organisation and management — 20
7. Methods of communication — 23
8. Motivating employees — 26
   Case study — 29

SECTION 3 Marketing
9. Marketing and the market — 32
10. Market research — 35
11. The marketing mix: product — 38
12. The marketing mix: price — 40
13. The marketing mix: place — 43
14. The marketing mix: promotion — 45
15. Ecommerce — 48
16. Marketing strategy, entering new markets in other countries and legal controls — 50
    Case study — 53

SECTION 4 Operations management
17. Production of goods and services — 56
18. Technology and production of goods and services — 58
19. Sustainable production of goods and services — 60
20. Costs, scale of production and break-even analysis — 62
21. Quality of goods and services — 66
22. Location decisions — 68
    Case study — 71

SECTION 5 Financial information and decisions
23. Business finance — 74
24. Cash flow forecast — 77
25. Profit and loss — 80
26. Statement of financial position — 83
27. Analysis of accounts — 85
    Case study — 88

SECTION 6 External influences on business activity
28. Economic issues — 91
29. Business and the international economy — 94
30. Business and the environment — 97
31. Business and ethical issues, and pressure groups — 99
    Case study — 101

1 Understanding business activity

Student Book Chapters 1–4

1 Business activity and economic sectors

Farah opened her business, Farah's Salon (FS), just after leaving school. She offers hairdressing and beauty services for women. She employs 3 workers who have quite different skills: 1 is a hair stylist, 1 is a beauty specialist and the other is a receptionist. This means that Farah is able to offer a wide range of beauty and hairdressing services very efficiently. Shampoos, hairsprays and many other beauty products are bought from several suppliers. Farah's business is now very busy. She is planning to use some of FS's capital to buy IT equipment to keep customer records of treatments they have received and to allow an accurate record of appointments to be kept.

Farah is keen to increase the added value of her business. She has not yet decided on the best way to do this. She thinks that redecorating the salon to give it a unique style will improve its image with customers and could allow her to increase prices.

FS operates in Country X. The business uses several suppliers to obtain all the materials, furniture and other equipment it needs. FS is in the tertiary sector and depends on other businesses in this sector for important services.

1 a Define 'factors of production'. *[2 marks]*

....

....

....

   b Outline **two** different factors of production used by Farah. *[4 marks]*

....

....

....

....

....

....

c Explain **one** secondary sector and **one** tertiary sector business used by Farah. [6 marks]

....
....
....
....
....
....
....
....

d Do you think redecoration of the salon is the best way for FS to increase added value? Justify your answer. [8 marks]

....
....
....
....
....
....
....
....
....
....
....

1 UNDERSTANDING BUSINESS ACTIVITY

2 Enterprise, business growth and size

Farah is very ambitious and she wants to expand her business quickly, although she is aware that many businesses fail, especially in their first few years. She works long hours and her commitment as an entrepreneur is a good example to her employees. She likes taking important decisions by herself. Her many ideas for expanding the business include offering a wider range of services to male customers as well as female. FS now employs 10 workers. The average sized business in hairdressing and beauty employs 5 workers. The total value of FS sales this year increased by 15%. Farah believes that FS has more advanced equipment – such as saunas and steam baths – than local competitors.

Farah is considering both internal growth and external growth for FS. She could open a new hair and beauty salon in another part of the city. She also knows about 2 other businesses for sale. Business A is a men's hairdressing salon that has been trading for many years. The owner is retiring and wants to sell quickly. Business B is a specialist producer of handmade organic cosmetics. FS uses some of these in the salon and they are very popular. The owner is ill and no longer wants the stress of harvesting natural products and meeting production deadlines. Farah wants to draw up a new business plan to help guide her through the next expansion stage of FS.

1 a Define 'internal growth'. *[2 marks]*

....

....

....

  b Outline **two** important characteristics that make Farah a successful entrepreneur. *[4 marks]*

....

....

....

....

....

....

  c Explain **two** ways the business plan drawn up by Farah will help when she expands the business. *[6 marks]*

....

....

....

....

....

....

....

2 Enterprise, business growth and size

d Do you think internal growth or external growth should be used by FS to expand? Justify your answer. *[8 marks]*

....

....

....

....

....

....

....

....

....

....

2 a Define 'business plan'. *[2 marks]*

....

....

....

b Outline **two** ways the size of FS could be compared to similar businesses. *[4 marks]*

....

....

....

....

....

....

1 UNDERSTANDING BUSINESS ACTIVITY

c Explain **two** possible business problems Farah might experience as she expands FS. *[6 marks]*

....

....

....

....

....

....

....

....

d Farah has decided to use external growth to expand FS. Do you think she should take over Business A or Business B? Justify your answer. *[8 marks]*

....

....

....

....

....

....

....

....

....

....

....

3 Types of business organisations

Farah set up Farah's Salon (FS) as a sole trader. She financed the start-up with her own savings and loans from her parents and her bank. As she is planning further growth for the business, she has been advised to take on at least 1 partner. Alternatively, she could convert the business to a private limited company in which the shareholders would benefit from limited liability. A friend has some savings he has offered to invest and become a partner in FS. He has no business experience and is often on holiday. A business consultant who advises Farah has suggested that his wife could become a partner in FS. He told Farah: 'She has savings to invest, is an experienced businessperson and likes being in control.'

Furniture for the salon is supplied by a large private limited company. It is owned by a wealthy family that considered converting the business into a public limited company 3 years ago. The family decided not to change because of the disadvantages of this form of business organisation.

Farah has been asked by a large national chain of beauty salons – called Spa Town – if she is interested in buying some of its salons that are operating as part of the franchise. It would give FS national advertising coverage but Spa Town would insist on changes to the way Farah operates her business. Farah has rejected this offer.

There is a manufacturer of hair products from another country that is planning to expand near FS. It has approached FS to see if Farah would like to form a joint venture. She is undecided whether to do this.

1 a Define 'franchise'. *[2 marks]*

   b Outline **two** disadvantages to Farah of being a sole trader. *[4 marks]*

1 UNDERSTANDING BUSINESS ACTIVITY

c Explain **one** advantage and **one** disadvantage to Farah of forming a business partnership. *[6 marks]*

....

....

....

....

....

....

....

....

d Do you think Farah should expand FS by buying existing salons operating as Spa Town franchises? Justify your answer. *[8 marks]*

....

....

....

....

....

....

....

....

....

....

2 a Define 'limited liability'. *[2 marks]*

....

....

....

3 Types of business organisations

b Outline **two** possible reasons why the furniture company did not convert its business into a public limited company. *[4 marks]*

c Explain **two** reasons why forming a private limited company would not be suitable for FS at the present time. *[6 marks]*

d Do you think Farah should form a joint venture with the business from another country? Justify your answer. *[8 marks]*

1 UNDERSTANDING BUSINESS ACTIVITY

4 Business objectives and stakeholder objectives

Farah's business objective has changed since she started Farah's Salon (FS) several years ago. It is now a private limited company which means that FS must keep the owners satisfied with a return on their investment.

FS now owns several salons in Main City. Farah plans to completely redevelop one of these sites. She wants to remove the existing building and construct a large apartment block in its place. The lower level will contain a newly equipped beauty salon and gymnasium. The gymnasium will allow FS to enter the fitness market for the first time and will appeal to men and women. There will be many new job opportunities. The redevelopment will take 6 months. Local residents are not happy about the plans. Some FS customers think that prices will be higher to make sure a profit is made. Farah told some senior managers: 'All stakeholders will benefit from the expansion of FS.' Farah's plans for business growth will be expensive and some shareholders are worried about the cost. They would prefer Farah to concentrate on making the existing salons more profitable. Farah could also aim to increase FS's market share.

1 a Define 'external stakeholder'. *[2 marks]*

b Identify **four** external stakeholder groups for FS. *[4 marks]*

c Explain **two** ways in which one stakeholder group, apart from employees, might be affected by plans to redevelop one of the salons. *[6 marks]*

4 Business objectives and stakeholder objectives

d Do you think it is right for Farah to say that 'all stakeholders will benefit from the expansion of FS'? Justify your answer. *[8 marks]*

....

....

....

....

....

....

....

....

....

....

2 a Identify the formula to calculate market share. *[2 marks]*

....

....

....

b Outline **two** likely objectives Farah set for FS when it was first established. *[4 marks]*

....

....

....

....

....

....

1 UNDERSTANDING BUSINESS ACTIVITY

c Explain **two** different business objectives that FS will now have after trading for several years. *[6 marks]*

....
....
....
....
....
....
....
....

d Do you think that the objectives of customers will always conflict with the objectives of shareholders? Justify your answer. *[8 marks]*

....
....
....
....
....
....
....
....
....

Understanding business activity: end-of-section case study

Use all the information at the start of the questions for Chapters 1, 2, 3 and 4 to help you answer the following question.

1 **a** Explain **two** advantages and **two** disadvantages for FS of continued growth of the business. [8 marks]
  b Farah wants to expand FS. Consider the advantages of each of the following methods of expansion. Which method should she choose? Justify your answer. [12 marks]
    i Redevelop existing salon including a new gymnasium.
    ii Sell FS franchise to other businesses.
    iii Take over another hairdressing and beauty salon business.

a ....

b ....

1 UNDERSTANDING BUSINESS ACTIVITY

2 People in business

Student Book Chapters 5–8

5 Human resource management (HRM)

Ice Cream Company (ICC) owns 16 ice cream cafes and has 1 factory that produces all the ice cream that ICC sells. The business is based in Country X. Sasha is the Managing Director. Each cafe employs 6 workers.

Asif, the Operations Manager, has decided to retire in 6 months' time. A new Operations Manager needs to be recruited. Sasha prefers to use internal recruitment for senior positions. The Human Resource (HR) Manager has pointed out that most of the junior managers in the factory have had no production experience other than with ICC. Sasha has agreed to consider external applicants too. She has posted an advertisement for the position on the company website.

Employees in the ICC cafes are worried about their job security. Another ice cream business has failed and several jobs have been lost. They do not yet have a written employment contract and changes in the law will soon make this a legal requirement. Several new employees have been recruited to replace employees who have left. Sasha told the HR Manager: 'We can give them some induction training. Then they can quickly learn on the job. This will be better than attending courses in food hygiene and customer service at the local college.'

1 a Define 'internal recruitment'. *[2 marks]*

....

....

....

b Outline **two** pieces of information that should be included in the job advertisement for the Operations Manager. *[4 marks]*

....

....

....

....

....

....

2 PEOPLE IN BUSINESS

   c Explain **two** selection methods that could be used to recruit the new Operations Manager. *[6 marks]*

   d Do you think external recruitment is the best method to use for a new Operations Manager? Justify your answer. *[8 marks]*

2 a Define 'induction training'. *[2 marks]*

5 Human resource management (HRM)

b Outline **two** legal controls over employment issues that might affect ICC. [4 marks]

c Explain **two** reasons why training employees is important to ICC. [6 marks]

d Do you think newly recruited cafe employees should be trained using on-the-job or off-the-job training? Justify your answer. [8 marks]

2 PEOPLE IN BUSINESS

6 Organisation and management

Sasha has designed a simple organisational structure for Ice Cream Company (ICC). Part of this is shown in Figure 6.1 below.

Cafe managers often complain that they are told about important decisions several days after the decisions have been made. They also think they should make decisions about employee hours, flexible working and which ice cream flavours to order. ICC's senior managers have clearly defined roles and can only act on important issues with Sasha's agreement. Sasha takes all major decisions within ICC. She does not like delegating authority to other managers. She is preparing the business for expansion into another city in Country X (where ICC is based). Sasha is working hard to make sure that all departments within ICC are ready for the opening of 3 new cafes in this location. Some potential competitors in this city have plans to reduce the size of their workforces.

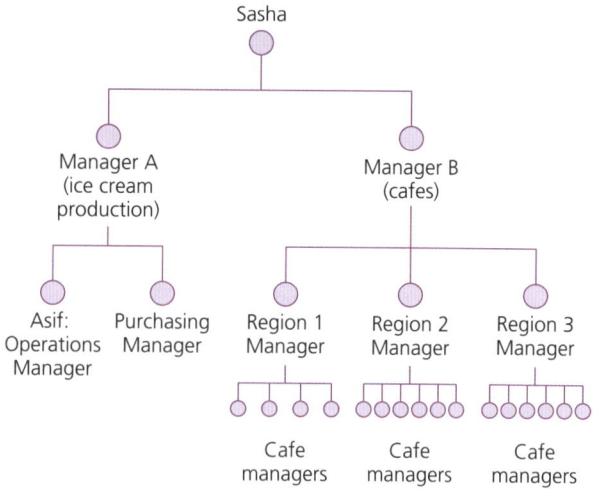

Figure 6.1: Organisational chart for ICC

The ICC factory is currently managed by Asif. He started at the factory as a young man and has worked in all parts of the factory. He thinks he knows the best way for each employee to perform their duties. He does not expect employees to show initiative. He wants to solve all problems his way. When he was away on holiday last month, the factory stopped production completely. No one knew how to solve a mechanical breakdown in 1 of the machines. ICC factory employees report directly to their supervisors. At a recent meeting of employees, someone suggested that they should all join a trade union.

1 a Identify the span of control for: *[2 marks]*

   Manager A: ....

   Manager B: ....

   b Outline **two** likely advantages to ICC of reducing the chain of command within the business. *[4 marks]*

   ....

   ....

   ....

   ....

   ....

   ....

6 Organisation and management

c Explain **two** functions of management performed by Sasha. [6 marks]

....

....

....

....

....

....

....

....

d Do you think Sasha should delegate some tasks to others below her in the hierarchy?
   Justify your answer. [8 marks]

....

....

....

....

....

....

....

....

....

....

....

2 a Identify **two** advantages of having a 'simple organisational structure'. [2 marks]

....

....

....

2 PEOPLE IN BUSINESS

b Outline **two** advantages of ICC introducing flexible working. *[4 marks]*

....

....

....

....

....

....

c Explain **two** advantages to ICC factory employees of joining a trade union. *[6 marks]*

....

....

....

....

....

....

....

....

....

d Do you think that using a democratic leadership style for factory employees would benefit ICC? Justify your answer. *[8 marks]*

....

....

....

....

....

....

....

....

....

....

7 Methods of communication

Asif has now retired and ICC's new Operations Manager has decided to stop using the noticeboard to communicate with employees. It leads to groups of employees talking about messages in the corridor. She does not think this method of internal communication is helpful. Communication barriers can be a problem for businesses.

The new Operations Manager used to work for a social media business. She has suggested to Sasha that internal communications within ICC – in the cafes and the factory – could be improved by using electronic methods of communication with each manager and employee. The Operations Manager also needs to communicate with external groups.

Sasha uses email to communicate with senior managers. She is encouraging them to use this method of communication with cafe managers too. Sasha has recently received 2 letters from customers. The first letter was a complaint about waiting times in an ICC cafe. The other was a compliment for the excellent quality of the ice creams. Both customers stated that there seemed to be no other obvious way of contacting the company other than by letter and one of the customers stated that 'the ICC telephone is never answered'. The other customer stated that when she complained about long waiting times to a cafe employee, she was not sure if the message was passed on to senior management.

The manager in one of the cafes has just started using daily 5-minute team briefings with his employees before the cafe opens. He has been surprised at the positive response from the cafe employees to this idea. The manager wondered whether or not he should tell Sasha about his idea.

1   a   Identify **two** disadvantages of using phone calls. *[2 marks]*

    ....
    ....
    ....

    b   Outline **two** examples of when ICC's Operations Manager will need to communicate with external groups. *[4 marks]*

    ....
    ....
    ....
    ....
    ....
    ....

2 PEOPLE IN BUSINESS

c Explain **two** possible communication barriers between ICC and its customers. [6 marks]

....

....

....

....

....

....

....

....

d Do you think that ICC should communicate with employees using only electronic methods? Justify your answer. [8 marks]

....

....

....

....

....

....

....

....

....

....

....

2 a Identify **two** advantages of using noticeboards. [2 marks]

....

....

....

7 Methods of communication

b Outline **one** advantage and **one** disadvantage of ICC cafe managers using meetings to communicate with employees. *[4 marks]*

....
....
....
....
....
....

c Explain **two** advantages to ICC of using email as a form of communication. *[6 marks]*

....
....
....
....
....
....
....
....

d Do you think that ICC should use the same method of communication in all situations? Justify your answer. *[8 marks]*

....
....
....
....
....
....
....
....
....

2 PEOPLE IN BUSINESS

8 Motivating employees

City Cafe is a typical ICC cafe with 6 employees. 3 of the employees are students who are unlikely to stay with the company for long. The other 3 workers have been employees of ICC for several years. 1 of the student employees left City Cafe recently. She said that there was no job satisfaction for her. However, other employees at the cafe disagreed. The employees in most ICC cafes make a well-motivated and effective team, working together and rotating the jobs between themselves. They are paid an hourly rate slightly above the legal minimum wage and this increases for each year of service.

Sasha wants to change the financial methods of motivation for employees. She plans to reduce the hourly wage rate for all cafe employees and offer a commission based on the number of customers each cafe serves each week. 'It should be possible, if sales increase, for employees to earn more each week than they do at present', she told her Human Resource Manager.

ICC factory employees are paid an hourly wage rate plus a bonus for meeting production targets. This can cause inventory problems during winter months. Each employee has 1 well-defined task to do and there is no opportunity for job enrichment. There is high labour turnover in the factory. The Operations Manager thinks that non-financial methods of motivation might be more effective than financial methods in keeping employees at ICC.

1 a Define 'motivation'. *[2 marks]*

....

....

....

b Outline **two** advantages to ICC of having a well-motivated workforce in its cafes. *[4 marks]*

....

....

....

....

....

....

c Explain **one** advantage to employees in the cafes and **one** advantage to employees in the factory of the current methods of payment. *[6 marks]*

....

....

....

....

....

....

....

d Do you think the cafe business should change from paying its employees an hourly rate to some other financial method of motivation? Justify your answer. [8 marks]

....

2 a Define 'job enrichment'. [2 marks]

....

b Outline **two** reasons why people work at ICC's factory. [4 marks]

....

2 PEOPLE IN BUSINESS

c Explain **one** advantage and **one** disadvantage of the bonus system currently used at ICC's factory. *[6 marks]*

....

....

....

....

....

....

....

....

d Do you think ICC should increase wage rates or use non-financial methods of motivation for employees? Justify your answer. *[8 marks]*

....

....

....

....

....

....

....

....

....

....

People in business: end-of-section case study

Use all the information at the start of the questions for Chapters 5, 6, 7 and 8 to help you answer the following questions.

1 a Explain **two** reasons why it is important to have good managers in each ICC cafe. [8 marks]

  b ICC is expanding and wants to open another cafe. Consider the following **three** ways Sasha could recruit new employees for the cafe. Which way should Sasha use? Justify your answer. [12 marks]

  i Ask existing employees if they know of anyone who is suitable.

  ii Advertise on an online recruitment site.

  iii Put up posters in existing ICC cafes.

a ....

b ....

2 PEOPLE IN BUSINESS

2 a Explain **two** examples of financial methods of motivation and **two** examples of non-financial methods of motivation that ICC could use. [8 marks]

b Consider the advantages and disadvantages of having only full-time employees or only part-time employees in the cafes. Which type of employees should ICC employ? Justify your answer. [12 marks]

a

b

3 Marketing

Student Book Chapters 9–16

9 Marketing and the market

The Drone Company (TDC) builds drones for customers who fly them for pleasure and to take part in competitions. Drones are small, remote-controlled powered vehicles that can take off and land vertically, and fly a considerable distance. TDC was started by Jez in his garage, but it now employs 25 production workers and has a small team of people in the Marketing department. Jez knows that the role of marketing is very important to TDC.

TDC aims to sell to niche markets such as:

- wedding photographers who can use the drones, fitted with cameras, to take amazing 'overhead' pictures of weddings
- enthusiasts who like specialised drone designs, unusual colours and powerful engines to use in competitions.

Mass markets were rejected by Jez as soon as he started TDC and his approach to segmenting the market seems to have led to high levels of customer loyalty.

Prices of standard drone models with no special features have fallen as more competitors have entered the market. The market is also affected by government regulation and technological developments in the engines that are used in drones.

Sales of TDC drones have continued to be high despite increasing competition. Ted is a senior TDC manager. Ted is so certain of the success of TDC models that he told Jez: 'The Marketing department is a waste of time because TDC drones are good quality products.'

1 a Identify **two** roles of marketing. *[2 marks]*

b Outline **two** possible effects on TDC of future changes in the market for its products. *[4 marks]*

9 Marketing and the market

c Explain **two** ways in which TDC could respond to increased competition. *[6 marks]*

....

....

....

....

....

....

....

....

d Do you think that TDC is right to concentrate on niche markets? Justify your answer. *[8 marks]*

....

....

....

....

....

....

....

....

....

....

2 a Define 'marketing'. *[2 marks]*

....

....

....

3 MARKETING

b Outline **two** ways in which TDC could try to maintain its competitiveness. *[4 marks]*

....

....

....

....

....

....

c Explain **one** advantage and **one** disadvantage of TDC segmenting the market. *[6 marks]*

....

....

....

....

....

....

....

....

d Do you agree with Ted who says that 'The Marketing department is a waste of time because TDC drones are good quality products'? Justify your answer. *[8 marks]*

....

....

....

....

....

....

....

....

10 Market research

Before Jez set up TDC, he searched online for drone manufacturers in Country X, where he lives. He was surprised by how few there were. After several years of success, Jez now wants to develop even more advanced drone models. He thinks there are market segments that have not yet been reached by TDC or other drone makers. TDC's Marketing Manager has suggested using only secondary market research, as TDC will not be able to contact everyone interested in buying a drone. Jez disagrees and thinks that all future TDC market research should use primary market research methods. Results of this market research could then be analysed after presenting it in tables and pie charts.

Jez also wants to find out what existing customers think of the TDC products they have bought. Jez believes that feedback from customers, in the form of a focus group, for example, could give TDC useful information. This might help to improve TDC products and customer service.

Ted thinks that market research is a waste of time in such a fast-changing market. He suggests spending more on new products and less on market research, which he says 'can become quickly outdated and inaccurate'.

1 a Identify **two** reasons why TDC might want to carry out market research. *[2 marks]*

....

....

....

b State **four** disadvantages of using secondary market research. *[4 marks]*

....

....

....

....

....

....

c Explain **two** reasons why TDC would have to use sampling if it undertakes primary market research. *[6 marks]*

....

....

....

....

....

....

....

....

3 MARKETING

d Do you think that TDC should spend money on market research or new products? Justify your answer. *[8 marks]*

....

....

....

....

....

....

....

....

....

2 a Define 'focus group'. *[2 marks]*

....

....

....

b Outline **two** questions that Jez could ask a focus group of TDC customers. *[4 marks]*

....

....

....

....

....

....

c Explain **one** advantage and **one** disadvantage to TDC of using a focus group to gather market research. *[6 marks]*

....

....

....

....

....

....

....

....

d Do you agree that all market research for TDC should be primary market research? Justify your answer. *[8 marks]*

....

....

....

....

....

....

....

....

....

....

....

3 MARKETING

11 The marketing mix: product

TDC offers customers a 'customising' service. This means that any drone ordered can be painted a colour the customer chooses and built with a wide variety of features and engine sizes. Jez thinks that this service is TDC's unique selling point (USP). There are currently 6 basic models in the company's product portfolio, all of which can be adapted to meet customer needs. The sales of the 'Tree Skimmer' have just started to fall. It was one of the first models produced by TDC. Sales of the 'Sky Buzz' are increasing rapidly – it has only been on the market for 2 weeks.

Ted wants to try to adapt the Tree Skimmer by adding some new features. He also plans to use a new social media promotion campaign for this model and update the packaging. Jez thinks that the company would be better advised to stop producing this product and work hard on developing a much-improved model that can replace the Tree Skimmer. TDC is now widely recognised as a main brand in the market for drones. Other competitors do not have the same strong brand image.

1 a Identify which stage of their product life cycles the following products are at:

    i Tree Skimmer   *[1 mark]*

    ii Sky Buzz   *[1 mark]*

b Outline **two** advantages to TDC of using extension strategies.   *[4 marks]*

11 The marketing mix: product

c Explain **two** advantages to TDC of having a recognised brand image. *[6 marks]*

d Do you think TDC should develop new products or try to extend the product life cycle of existing products? Justify your answer. *[8 marks]*

3 MARKETING

12 The marketing mix: price

A new competitor has just entered the drone market in Country X. It is selling a drone model at a price much lower than any of TDC's prices. 'This is an example of penetration pricing,' Jez told his managers.

The Marketing Manager has been discussing with Jez the best cost-plus price to charge for the latest TDC drone model, the 'Typhoon', to be launched next month. 'I have estimated the average cost of making each unit of this model is $220. If we add a mark-up of 50%, that will be more expensive than competitors' prices, but they do not have our strong brand image,' he told Jez.

The new model could be sold online. TDC is not selling any of its products online at present but is considering using dynamic pricing if it starts to sell online in the future.

1 a Calculate the cost-plus price for the Typhoon model from the information given. *[2 marks]*

....
....
....

b Outline **two** reasons why pricing decisions are important to TDC. *[4 marks]*

....
....
....
....
....
....

c Explain **one** advantage and **one** disadvantage of dynamic pricing to TDC. *[6 marks]*

....
....
....
....
....
....
....
....

12 The marketing mix: price

d Do you think TDC should use price skimming for all new models of specialised products that it develops? Justify your answer. *[8 marks]*

2 a Define 'cost-plus pricing'. *[2 marks]*

b Outline **one** advantage and **one** disadvantage to TDC if it starts to use penetration pricing. *[4 marks]*

3 MARKETING

c Explain **one** advantage and **one** disadvantage to TDC of using cost-plus pricing. *[6 marks]*

....

....

....

....

....

....

....

....

d Do you think TDC should use different pricing methods for each of its products? Justify your answer. *[8 marks]*

....

....

....

....

....

....

....

....

....

....

13 The marketing mix: place

TDC sells most of its drones directly to customers. Potential customers contact TDC and ask for a brochure and price list. Other customers use the company's website to obtain information and then order by telephone or visit the TDC shop and purchase their drone in person. The TDC website does not currently allow orders to be placed online. Jez enjoys meeting as many customers as possible, as this allows him to get to know their particular requirements, including the features of the products that are most in demand.

Drones are technical products and Jez has never trusted shops to employ staff who could explain the detailed designs and methods of operation of his company's products. As TDC's sales increase, Jez realises that the distribution channels the company uses need to adapt and change. Ted wants to talk to a specialist retailer of drones and electronic equipment. He wants to ask what discount it would need from the normal selling price to sell TDC's models through its shops. Ted could also choose to sell through wholesalers.

1 a Define 'retailer'. *[2 marks]*

....

....

....

b Outline **two** advantages to TDC of selling directly to customers. *[4 marks]*

....

....

....

....

....

....

c Explain **one** advantage and **one** disadvantage to TDC of selling through wholesalers. *[6 marks]*

....

....

....

....

....

....

....

3 MARKETING

d Do you think specialist retailers are the best way for TDC to distribute its products? Justify your answer. *[8 marks]*

14 The marketing mix: promotion

Although TDC has an excellent reputation, the company still needs to have a plan for promotion of its products. New products are being launched frequently – the Typhoon model, which can fly at a very high speed, is being sold for the first time next month. In addition, some of the existing models need a boost to their sales at certain times of the year or when they are approaching the end of the maturity phase of their product life cycles.

It has been decided to try to maintain sales of the Tree Skimmer model for a few more months, so the Marketing Manager is thinking about which methods of sales promotion would be most suitable. Other methods of extending the life of this product are also being considered. TDC spends about 10% of total revenue on advertising and sales promotion.

Ted told Jez: 'Our products have now got such a strong following from a loyal group of customers that TDC should immediately stop all promotion. Sales will not fall if we use the money saved to invest in new products.'

1 a Define 'promotion'. *[2 marks]*

b Outline **two** aims that Jez could establish for the promotion used by TDC. *[4 marks]*

c Explain **two** methods of sales promotion that TDC could use for the Tree Skimmer model. *[6 marks]*

3 MARKETING

d Do you agree with Ted that TDC should stop all promotion completely? Justify your answer. *[8 marks]*

....
....
....
....
....
....
....
....
....
....

2 a Identify **two** factors that affect which method of advertising is chosen. *[2 marks]*

....
....
....

b Outline **two** reasons why TDC advertises. *[4 marks]*

....
....
....
....
....
....

c Explain **two** advertising methods that TDC could use for the Typhoon model. [6 marks]

....

....

....

....

....

....

....

....

d Do you think that increased advertising is the best way to extend the life cycle of TDC's existing products? Justify your answer. [8 marks]

....

....

....

....

....

....

....

....

....

....

....

3 MARKETING

15 Ecommerce

Jez is keen to see that the business objective of growth is met. He said: 'I think we should only use social media and online methods for our promotion in future. Do you really think the majority of our potential customers are at home watching TV most evenings? I also think that just using ecommerce to sell and distribute the drones would fit in much better with TDC's technological image, especially among young customers. We should also sell new models using online shopping to cut out profits being made by other distribution businesses.'

The Marketing Manager disagreed and said: 'Many companies buy our commercial drones and parents often buy the cheaper drones for their children. Many customers like to see our products before they buy them. We need to have a flexible approach to promotion and ecommerce.'

1 a Define 'online shopping'. *[2 marks]*

....

....

....

b Outline **two** advantages to TDC's customers of using ecommerce. *[4 marks]*

....

....

....

....

....

....

15 Ecommerce

c Explain **two** likely advantages of ecommerce to TDC. [6 marks]

....

....

....

....

....

....

....

....

d Do you agree that TDC should only sell its new models using ecommerce? Justify your answer. [8 marks]

....

....

....

....

....

....

....

....

....

....

3 MARKETING

16 Marketing strategy, entering new markets in other countries and legal controls

TDC has now been operating for 5 years. The drone market in Country X is no longer growing. TDC's market share is stable. Jez plans to start exporting the latest TDC drone models to other countries. In Country Y, it used to be illegal to sell drones but the government has recently changed legal controls and drones can now be sold. Anyone purchasing a drone needs a licence first and there are other legal controls which cover drone safety and a minimum age limit for consumers.

'There is a great potential new market in Country Y,' Jez told his senior managers. 'If we get the marketing strategy right and use a suitable marketing mix, we can be as successful there as in our own country.' Ted agreed but suggested that Country Y's consumers were likely to have different requirements from those in Country X. Ted said, 'Incomes are lower on average and we need to know which groups of people are going to be allowed to buy drones. If we make mistakes with our product launch in Country Y, for example, by advertising to children, we could get some bad publicity.'

1 a Define 'marketing strategy'. *[2 marks]*

....

....

....

b Outline **two** factors, other than the marketing objectives, that will affect the marketing strategy TDC uses in Country Y. *[4 marks]*

....

....

....

....

....

....

c Explain **two** reasons why TDC wants to enter new markets in Country Y. *[6 marks]*

....

....

....

....

....

....

....

16 Marketing strategy, entering new markets in other countries and legal controls

d Do you think the marketing strategy used in Country Y will need to be different from the marketing strategy used in Country X? Justify your answer. *[8 marks]*

....

....

....

....

....

....

....

....

....

....

....

2 a Identify **two** elements of the marketing mix that are part of the marketing strategy. *[2 marks]*

....

....

....

b Outline **two** possible effects of legal controls on TDC's marketing mix. *[4 marks]*

....

....

....

....

....

....

3 MARKETING

c Explain **two** possible advantages to TDC of selling in markets in other countries. *[6 marks]*

....
....
....
....
....
....
....
....

d Consider **two** ways TDC might overcome the disadvantages of entering a new market in Country Y. Which would be the best one to use? Justify your answer. *[8 marks]*

....
....
....
....
....
....
....
....
....
....
....
....

Marketing: end-of-section case study

Use all the information at the start of the questions for Chapters 9, 10, 11, 12, 13, 14, 15 and 16 to help you answer the following questions.

1 a Explain **one** advantage and **one** disadvantage of using interviews to find out the needs of new customers. [8 marks]

  b Consider whether TDC should develop a cheaper product aimed at the mass market or continue to develop niche market products. Which is the best option to choose? Justify your answer. [12 marks]

a ......

b ......

3 MARKETING

2 a Explain **two** factors to consider when designing the packaging for the drones. [8 marks]

b TDC has developed a new product which is a small, low-flying drone that only flies at low speeds and is easy to handle. Consider each of the following **three** elements of the marketing mix for the new drone to be marketed to children. Which element of the marketing mix would you change to make the marketing mix more successful? Justify your answer. [12 marks]

- Pricing method is competitive.
- Promotion is using competitions and billboards.
- Place – the model is only to be sold through large toy shops.

b

4 Operations management

Student Book Chapters 17–22

17 Production of goods and services

Benson Clearwater Clothing (BCC) is a private limited company that manufactures a range of clothing for men, women and children. It is located in Main City in Country X. It manufactures clothing using traditional labour-intensive methods of production.

BCC has high labour productivity with well-qualified and skilled employees. They are well-paid and well-motivated. Most of the workforce has worked for BCC for many years. Electric cutting machines and electric sewing machines are used to produce high-quality clothes. BCC purchases cloth from suppliers in Country X.

BCC uses batch production and holds high levels of cloth inventories, as well as finished items of clothing. However, the directors have been considering the concept of lean production and may introduce just-in-time (JIT) inventory control.

1 a State the formula to calculate labour productivity. *[2 marks]*

....

....

....

b Outline **two** reasons why efficiency is important to BCC. *[4 marks]*

....

....

....

....

....

....

17 Production of goods and services

c Explain **two** reasons why BCC uses batch production rather than flow production. [6 marks]

....

d Do you think that BCC should introduce just-in-time (JIT) inventory control into the factory? Justify your answer. [8 marks]

....

4 OPERATIONS MANAGEMENT

18 Technology and production of goods and services

BCC is considering introducing new technology into the factory to make production more efficient. The directors know that computer-aided manufacturing (CAM) can speed up the production process and reduce mistakes in the manufacture of its clothes. However, BCC knows that if it introduces new technology, it is likely to reduce the number of production employees it needs and the remaining workforce will need further training on how to use the new machinery.

BCC's bank has recently introduced new services using Artificial Intelligence (AI) chatbots. The chatbot can answer questions from customers and fewer employees are now needed in the Customer Service department. Banks are encouraging retailers to use contactless payment in their shops.

1 a Define 'computer-aided manufacturing (CAM)'. *[2 marks]*

....

....

....

b Outline **two** ways BCC's bank has increased productivity. *[4 marks]*

....

....

....

....

....

....

18 Technology and production of goods and services

c Explain **two** ways technology would affect the manufacture of clothes at BCC. [6 marks]

....
....
....
....
....
....
....
....

d Do you think production employees should encourage the business to invest in new technology to manufacture its products? Justify your answer. [8 marks]

....
....
....
....
....
....
....
....
....
....

4 OPERATIONS MANAGEMENT

19 Sustainable production of goods and services

The directors of BCC want the business to become more sustainable. They have been considering how BCC can reduce the waste created when producing clothing. A lot of waste cloth is left after the clothing design has been cut out of the fabric. The Operations Manager is trying to find ways to redesign the clothes so less waste is left over. The directors are also considering changing the cloth used in the production of the company's clothes. Fabric can be made from cotton that is grown using farming methods that are considered sustainable.

BCC may start to use renewable energy such as wind power. However, the cost of installing wind turbines is expensive and a suitable source of finance would be needed. The energy produced from wind power will be much cheaper than fossil fuels in the future.

One of the directors of BCC thinks that becoming sustainable is not necessary for clothing products as customers are only concerned with the style and price of their clothes. He thinks the costs of becoming more sustainable will reduce profit unless sales increase.

1 a Define 'renewable energy'. *[2 marks]*

   ....

   ....

   ....

   b Outline **two** ways, other than those referred to, in which BCC could become more sustainable. *[4 marks]*

   ....

   ....

   ....

   ....

   ....

   ....

c Explain **one** advantage and **one** disadvantage to BCC of the business becoming more sustainable. *[6 marks]*

d Do you agree with the director that becoming sustainable is not necessary for a clothing manufacturer as customers are only interested in the style and price of BCC's clothes? Justify your answer. *[8 marks]*

4 OPERATIONS MANAGEMENT

20 Costs, scale of production and break-even analysis

The Operations Manager at BCC has produced the following cost information for the bestselling item of women's clothing that BCC manufactures. At the existing factory, it can produce 1000 items per week at maximum output. However, if BCC moves to a new, larger factory, it can produce 4000 items of clothing per week. The selling price is $5 and BCC plans to keep the same price if it moves to the larger factory.

Table 20.1

Output	1000 per week (existing factory)	4000 per week (new factory)
Fixed costs	$1000	$4000
Variable cost per item of clothing	$2	$1

1 a Calculate the average cost of making one item of clothing in the new factory when at full capacity. *[2 marks]*

   b Outline **two** diseconomies of scale that BCC could experience if it moves to the new, larger factory. *[4 marks]*

20 Costs, scale of production and break-even analysis

c Explain **two** economies of scale that BCC could benefit from if it moves to the new, larger factory. [6 marks]

....
....
....
....
....
....
....
....

d Do you think BCC should reduce the price of its products if it moves to the new, larger factory? Justify your answer. [8 marks]

....
....
....
....
....
....
....
....
....
....
....

4 OPERATIONS MANAGEMENT

2 a Use the cost information provided (in the questions below and on page 62) and assume the selling price remains at $5. Complete the break-even chart below for BCC's item of women's clothing at the new, larger factory. *[4 marks]*

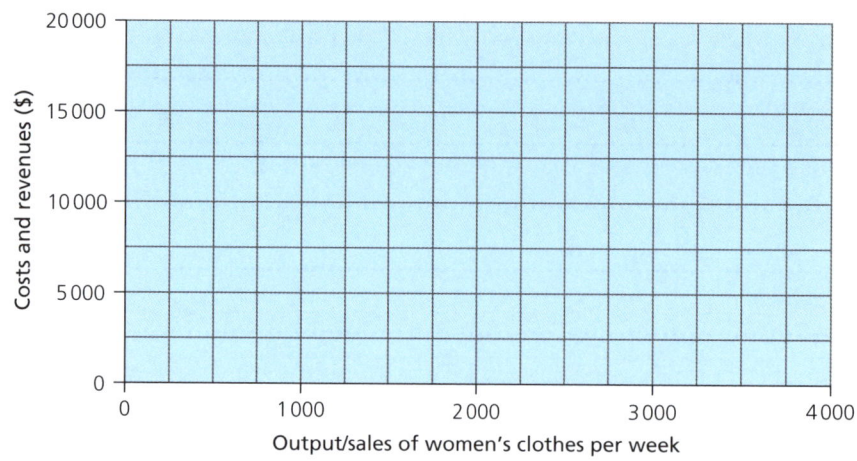

(Space for rough working) ....

....

....

....

....

....

b On your break-even chart, show the new break-even level of output if the variable cost increases to $2.50 per item. *[2 marks]*

(Space for rough working) ....

....

....

20 Costs, scale of production and break-even analysis

c Calculate the margin of safety at full capacity if the variable cost rises to $2.50 per item. *[2 marks]*

....

....

....

d Do you think BCC is right to use break-even analysis to help make decisions? Justify your answer. *[8 marks]*

....

....

....

....

....

....

....

....

....

....

4 OPERATIONS MANAGEMENT

21 Quality of goods and services

BCC uses quality control to check samples of the clothing items it has manufactured before they are sent to retailers and wholesalers. Most of the items of clothing are correctly made but occasionally there are mistakes and faulty items are sent to retailers and wholesalers. These faulty items are then returned to BCC for replacements.

1 a Identify **two** reasons why maintaining quality products is important to a business. *[2 marks]*

....
....
....

b Outline **two** advantages of using quality control for BCC. *[4 marks]*

....
....
....
....
....
....

c Explain **two** effects for BCC of sending out faulty items of clothing. *[6 marks]*

....
....
....
....
....
....
....
....
....

21 Quality of goods and services

d Do you think BCC should change from using quality control to quality assurance? Justify your answer. *[8 marks]*

....
....
....
....
....
....
....
....
....
....

4 OPERATIONS MANAGEMENT

22 Location decisions

The directors of BCC have decided to move all production to a larger factory in Country X. The following information on the map (Figure 22.1) is for two sites the company could buy. BCC is also considering opening a second factory in Country Z, where 75% of the clothes it produces are sold, or in another country where BCC wants to increase its sales.

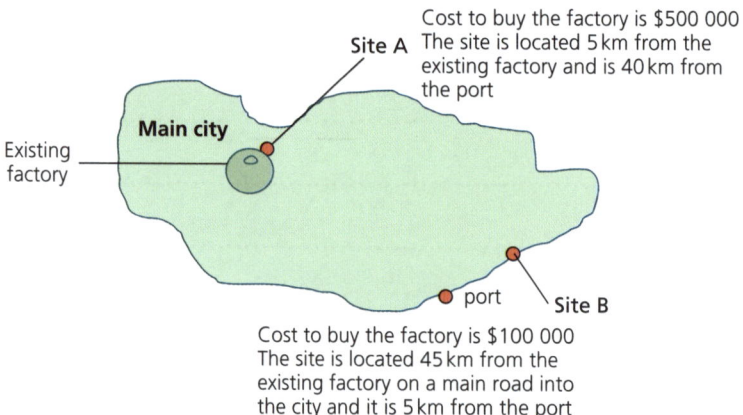

Figure 22.1: Map of two sites for sale in Country X

1 a Identify **two** examples of when location decisions are important to a business. *[2 marks]*

....

....

....

b Outline **two** factors that affect the location of a retailer of BCC products. *[4 marks]*

....

....

....

....

....

....

c Explain **two** factors that are likely to affect the location of the new BCC factory. *[6 marks]*

....

....

....

....

....

....

....

....

d Which site do you think BCC should buy? Justify your answer. *[8 marks]*

....

....

....

....

....

....

....

....

....

....

2 a Identify **two** ways governments influence location decisions. *[2 marks]*

....

....

....

4 OPERATIONS MANAGEMENT

b Outline **one** advantage and **one** disadvantage for a retailer selling BCC's products of being located near other similar shops. *[4 marks]*

....

....

....

....

....

....

c Explain **two** location factors influencing BCC's decision of which country to locate the second factory. *[6 marks]*

....

....

....

....

....

....

....

....

....

d The directors of BCC could decide to relocate all its production to Country Z and stop production in Country X. Do you think they should do this? Justify your answer. *[8 marks]*

....

....

....

....

....

....

....

....

....

Operations management: end-of-section case study

Use all the information at the start of the questions for Chapters 17, 18, 19, 20, 21 and 22 to help you answer the following questions.

1 **a** Explain **one** advantage and **one** disadvantage of using job production to produce a dress for a special customer. [8 marks]
   b Consider the following **two** ways BCC could improve productivity. Which **one** is the best one to use? Justify your answer. [12 marks]
   i Introduce automation and technology.
   ii Improve labour skills by training employees.

a ....

b ....

4 OPERATIONS MANAGEMENT

....

....

....

....

....

....

....

....

....

....

....

....

2 a Explain **two** reasons for an increase in the break-even level of output to cause concern for BCC's directors. [8 marks]
  b The directors of BCC want to become more sustainable. Consider the following **two** ways BCC could become more sustainable. Which way should BCC choose? Justify your answer. [12 marks]
   i Create less waste.
   ii Use renewable energy.

  a ....

....

....

....

....

....

....

....

....

b

5 Financial information and decisions

Student Book Chapters 23–27

23 Business finance

Ted set up his business as a sole trader 10 years ago in Country X. He had both internal and external sources of finance as he used his own savings and a bank loan to finance the start-up capital requirements and long-term capital requirements of equipment and vehicles for his taxi business. He decided not to consider crowdfunding or to take out an overdraft.

The business is located in Main City and has been very successful every year since it was started. Ted has retained some of his profit each year to reinvest back into the business.

Ted's Taxis (TT) now has 10 taxis, as Ted has bought a new taxi each year since the business started. Ted has now leased 2 trucks to expand his business into a different type of market. He wants to transport materials and finished goods for other businesses. However, this will mean he will have to wait a long time to be paid, as other businesses will expect to get trade credit arrangements from TT. Ted knows he must ensure he has enough working capital for the business. Ted wants to grow this other side of the business and is changing the business to a private limited company called Ted's Transport.

1 a Define 'retained profit'. *[2 marks]*

....
....
....

b Outline **one** advantage and **one** disadvantage for Ted if he had used crowdfunding to start his business. *[4 marks]*

....
....
....
....
....
....

23 Business finance

c Explain **two** factors that Ted's Bank Manager would have considered before giving him a bank loan to start his business. *[6 marks]*

....

....

....

....

....

....

....

....

d Do you think TT should arrange a bank overdraft for the business? Justify your answer. *[8 marks]*

....

....

....

....

....

....

....

....

....

....

2 a Define 'leasing'. *[2 marks]*

....

....

....

5 FINANCIAL INFORMATION AND DECISIONS

b Outline **one** advantage and **one** disadvantage to Ted of using trade credit. *[4 marks]*

....

....

....

....

....

....

c Explain **two** reasons why Ted needs finance to expand TT. *[6 marks]*

....

....

....

....

....

....

....

....

....

d Do you think TT, the private limited company, should take out a bank loan or issue more shares when expanding the business? Justify your answer. *[8 marks]*

....

....

....

....

....

....

....

....

24 Cash flow forecast

Ted has produced the outline of a cash flow forecast for TT, as shown in Table 24.1. For 3 months of the year the cash inflow becomes very low. During these months there are few tourists visiting the country and so demand for taxi services falls. However, the demand for trucks to transport goods is still high and stays the same all year round.

To operate the trucks as well as the taxis is expensive and the cash outflows are high all year round. The cost of leasing is high and has to be paid, whether the trucks are being used or not. The business customers who pay TT to transport their goods in trucks are given trade credit of 3 months in which to pay. Ted pays for fuel on 1 month's trade credit. All the taxi customers pay cash.

Table 24.1

$000	July	August	September	October	November	December
Cash inflow						
Cash from taxis	50	50	40	40	10	10
Payments received from transport customers	10	10	10	10	10	10
Capital and loans	–	–	200	–	–	–
Total cash inflows	A	60	250	50	20	20
Cash outflow						
Purchase of vehicles	–	–	–	D	–	–
Wages	20	20	20	20	10	10
Fuel	5	B	4	4	1	1
Other expenses	20	20	20	20	20	20
Total cash outflows	45	45	44	294	31	31
Net cash flow	15	15	206	(244)	E	(11)
Opening balance	10	25	C	246	2	(9)
Closing balance	25	40	246	2	(9)	F

1 a Define 'cash flow forecast'. *[2 marks]*

....

....

....

b Outline **one** advantage and **one** disadvantage for TT of drawing up a cash flow forecast. *[4 marks]*

....

....

....

....

....

5 FINANCIAL INFORMATION AND DECISIONS

c Complete the cash flow forecast (Table 24.1) by filling in A, B, C, D, E and F. [6 marks]

A ....

B ....

C ....

D ....

E ....

F ....

d Ted thinks he needs a large closing balance each month. Do you agree with him? Justify your answer. [8 marks]

....

....

....

....

....

....

....

....

....

2 a Define 'closing balance'. [2 marks]

....

....

....

24 Cash flow forecast

b Outline **two** examples of stakeholders who would be interested in TT's cash flow forecast. *[4 marks]*

....

....

....

....

....

....

c Explain **two** reasons why TT's cash flow forecast might need to be amended. *[6 marks]*

....

....

....

....

....

....

....

....

....

d Explain **two** ways a short-term cash flow problem could be overcome by TT. Which way is the best one to use? Justify your answer. *[8 marks]*

....

....

....

....

....

....

....

....

....

....

5 FINANCIAL INFORMATION AND DECISIONS

25 Profit and loss

When Ted changed the business into the private limited company Ted's Transport (TT), his family and friends bought shares in TT. The taxi part of the business is doing well but it still has 3 months in the year when the number of customers is reduced. The revenue from the truck transport part of the business has continued to increase as Ted has attracted many new customers from businesses located around Main City.

Ted has produced the following statements of profit or loss for this year and last year for his shareholders (Table 25.1). He thinks the performance of the business has improved but he is not sure. Ted plans to use the statements of profit or loss to help him make decisions.

Table 25.1

	Previous year ($000)	Current year ($000)
Revenue	400	500
Cost of sales	40	50
Gross profit	A	B
Expenses	320	400
Profit	C	D

1 a Define 'statement of profit or loss'. *[2 marks]*

b Calculate the figures for A, B, C and D in Table 25.1. *[4 marks]*

A ....
B ....
C ....
D ....

c Explain **two** reasons why making a profit is important to TT. *[6 marks]*

25 Profit and loss

d Do you think TT should focus on increasing profit or increasing revenue? Justify your answer. *[8 marks]*

....

....

....

....

....

....

....

....

....

....

2 a State the formula for calculating revenue. *[2 marks]*

....

....

....

b Outline **two** reasons why profit might have increased over the two years shown in TT's statements of profit or loss. *[4 marks]*

....

....

....

....

....

....

5 FINANCIAL INFORMATION AND DECISIONS

c Explain **two** reasons why stakeholders of TT would want to look at its statement of profit or loss. *[6 marks]*

....
....
....
....
....
....
....
....

d Do you think the directors of TT should reduce dividends or raise prices if they aim to increase retained profit? Justify your answer. *[8 marks]*

....
....
....
....
....
....
....
....
....
....

26 Statement of financial position

Ted has drawn up the following summary of the statement of financial position (Table 26.1) to show the Bank Manager. He wants to arrange an overdraft and obtain a new bank loan of $50 000. Ted intends to buy some new machinery that will allow him to carry out his own repairs to the taxis. This will benefit TT as it will not have to pay expensive garage repair costs.

Ted believes that keeping a high inventory of fuel is important so that TT never runs out of fuel for the taxis or trucks. TT still owns 10 taxi vehicles but the value of them has reduced as they are now old and this has reduced capital employed.

Table 26.1

ASSETS	$000s
Non-current assets	
Machinery	100
Vehicles	1000
Current assets	
Inventory	30
Trade receivables	20
Cash	10
Total assets	1160
LIABILITIES	
Current liabilities	
Trade payables	40
Overdraft	0
Non-current liabilities	
Long-term bank loan	100
Total liabilities	140
TOTAL ASSETS – TOTAL LIABILITIES	1020

1 a Define 'statement of financial position'. *[2 marks]*

....

....

....

b Outline the difference between an asset and a liability for TT. *[4 marks]*

....

....

....

....

....

....

c Explain **one** advantage and **one** disadvantage of TT holding a high level of inventory. *[6 marks]*

....

....

....

....

....

....

....

5 FINANCIAL INFORMATION AND DECISIONS

d Do you think Ted's decision to ask for an additional bank loan is a good one? Justify your answer. *[8 marks]*

27 Analysis of accounts

Ted uses the accounts and calculates profitability and liquidity ratios to see how well TT is performing. He has drawn up the following table showing TT's profitability and liquidity ratios for the last financial year (Table 27.1).

Ted also wants to compare TT with other businesses and has included the performance ratios for another business. Business A is a taxi business.

Table 27.1: Summary of financial information for TT and Business A

	TT	Business A
Profitability ratios		
Gross profit margin	90%	95%
Profit margin	10%	8%
Return on Capital Employed (ROCE)	4.5%	7%
Liquidity ratios		
Current ratio	1.5	1.0
Acid test ratio	0.75	0.9

1 a State the formula to calculate gross profit margin. [2 marks]

    ....

    ....

    ....

   b Outline **two** reasons why the gross profit margin of TT might fall. [4 marks]

    ....

    ....

    ....

    ....

    ....

    ....

5 FINANCIAL INFORMATION AND DECISIONS

c Explain **two** ways that Ted could improve the profit margin of TT. [6 marks]

....
....
....
....
....
....
....
....

d Do you think Ted should be satisfied with the profitability of TT compared with the other business shown in Table 27.1? Justify your answer. [8 marks]

....
....
....
....
....
....
....
....
....
....

2 a State the formula to calculate the current ratio. [2 marks]

....
....
....

27 Analysis of accounts

b Outline **two** reasons why TT's current ratio might be lower next year. *[4 marks]*

....

....

....

....

....

....

c Explain **one** advantage and **one** disadvantage of having a high acid test ratio. *[6 marks]*

....

....

....

....

....

....

....

....

....

d Do you think Ted should be satisfied with the liquidity of TT compared with the other business shown in Table 27.1? Justify your answer. *[8 marks]*

....

....

....

....

....

....

....

....

....

....

5 FINANCIAL INFORMATION AND DECISIONS

Financial information and decisions: end-of-section case study

Use the information below and at the start of the questions for Chapters 23, 24, 25, 26 and 27 to help you answer the following questions.

12 months have passed since the year shown in Table 27.1 (on page 85). At the end of this year, TT's accounts recorded:
- revenue of $600 000
- cost of sales of $30 000
- expenses of $520 000.

Its current assets are $62 500, of which inventory is $12 500 and current liabilities are $50 000.

1 a Explain **two** reasons why Ted will find a cash flow forecast useful. [8 marks]
   b Consider how the following **three** changes would affect TT's statement of profit or loss and statement of financial position. Which would have the greatest effect on the business? Justify your answer. [12 marks]
   - Ted takes out a bank loan to buy 2 new trucks.
   - Ted buys inventory only using trade credit.
   - There is an increase in the number of TT's taxi customers.

a ....

b ....

Financial information and decisions: end-of-section case study

2 a Explain **two** sources of internal finance and **two** sources of external finance that
Ted could use for TT. [8 marks]
b Refer to the financial information for TT provided on page 88 and the ratios for TT provided
in Table 27.1 (on page 85). Do you think Ted should be more worried about the profitability
or liquidity of TT? Justify your answer by calculating suitable ratios for TT. [12 marks]

a

5 FINANCIAL INFORMATION AND DECISIONS

b

6 External influences on business activity

Student Book Chapters 28–31

28 Economic issues

Abe's Best Cycles (ABC) produces motorbikes in Country X. The company was set up 50 years ago. The motorbikes are designed to meet the needs of low-income consumers in Country X.

ABC employs 500 skilled employees in its factory and uses capital-intensive production. 90% of all the motorbikes are sold in Country X. There are several other motorbike manufacturers in Country X but more than half of the motorbikes sold in Country X are imported. The competitors of ABC import 100% of their components while ABC imports only half of the components it needs. It buys the rest from local suppliers.

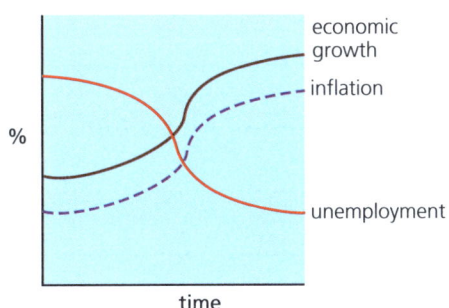

Figure 28.1

The economy of Country X has experienced economic growth after being in a recession. Unemployment is falling but the rate of inflation is starting to rise. The government is considering different ways to reduce inflation.

1 a Define 'unemployment'. *[2 marks]*

....

....

....

b Identify the **four** stages of the business cycle. *[4 marks]*

....

....

....

....

....

....

6 EXTERNAL INFLUENCES ON BUSINESS ACTIVITY

c Explain **two** problems for ABC that are likely to result from high levels of economic growth. *[6 marks]*

d Do you think falling unemployment will always benefit ABC? Justify your answer. *[8 marks]*

2 a Define 'economic growth'. *[2 marks]*

28 Economic issues

b Outline **two** possible effects on ABC of an increase in tax on business profits. *[4 marks]*

....

....

....

....

....

....

c Explain **one** advantage and **one** disadvantage to ABC from an increase in interest rates. *[6 marks]*

....

....

....

....

....

....

....

....

....

d Explain **two** likely effects on ABC from an increase in taxes on people's incomes. Which will have the greatest effect on ABC? Justify your answer. *[8 marks]*

....

....

....

....

....

....

....

....

....

6 EXTERNAL INFLUENCES ON BUSINESS ACTIVITY

29 Business and the international economy

There has been an appreciation of the exchange rate of Country X but not all businesses in Country X have benefitted from this. The competitors of ABC import all their components, while ABC imports only half of the components it needs.

The directors of ABC are planning to expand the business. ABC wants to start selling motorbikes in many other countries, such as Country Y. It knows that there are several reasons for globalisation and ABC may benefit in particular from free-trade agreements.

The directors want ABC to become a multinational company. The directors believe there are advantages from this change but they are not sure all the employees will benefit because additional production will be in factories in other countries. There are also external costs and benefits to ABC of locating factories in other countries, especially those that have areas of natural beauty and attract tourists.

The government of Country Y is encouraging multinational businesses to set up in its country. It believes that multinational businesses will help Country Y to become more developed and the country will benefit from more economic growth. The government believes the benefits from increased production from multinationals in Country Y will outweigh the disadvantages to some local businesses.

1 a Define 'multinational company'. *[2 marks]*

....

....

....

b Outline **two** opportunities to ABC from increased globalisation. *[4 marks]*

....

....

....

....

....

....

c Explain **two** advantages to ABC of becoming a multinational company. *[6 marks]*

....

....

....

....

....

....

....

d Do you think the government of a country should encourage more multinationals to set up in that country? Justify your answer. *[8 marks]*

....

....

....

....

....

....

....

....

....

....

2 a Define 'appreciation of an exchange rate'. *[2 marks]*

....

....

....

b Outline **two** ways that ABC might cause external costs. *[4 marks]*

....

....

....

....

....

....

6 EXTERNAL INFLUENCES ON BUSINESS ACTIVITY

c Explain **two** reasons why it might be easier for ABC to sell its products in Country X rather than to export them. *[6 marks]*

....

....

....

....

....

....

....

....

d Do you think ABC will benefit from an appreciation of Country X's exchange rate? Justify your answer. *[8 marks]*

....

....

....

....

....

....

....

....

....

....

30 Business and the environment

ABC is developing more energy-efficient motorbikes. These motorbikes produce less harmful gases from the exhaust and use less fuel (per kilometre). The government in Country X is introducing legal controls to restrict the amount of pollution produced in emissions from cars and motorbikes. Many other countries' governments are using similar controls to try to reduce the emissions of harmful greenhouse gases.

ABC is also considering using solar panels to generate electricity. The electricity generated will be used in the factory and it will reduce energy costs for ABC. However, the solar panels are expensive to buy and install.

The government is encouraging businesses to recycle and reduce waste during the manufacturing process. ABC is considering using recycled metals in the manufacture of new motorbikes.

Advert from the government

> **Protect the environment – fit solar panels to your factory roof**
> *The government will give you a grant towards the cost of installing solar panels. Your customers will appreciate this too!*

1 a Define 'pollution'. [2 marks]

....

....

....

b Outline **two** effects on ABC of the government of Country X introducing legal controls on emissions. [4 marks]

....

....

....

....

....

....

6 EXTERNAL INFLUENCES ON BUSINESS ACTIVITY

c Explain **one** advantage and **one** disadvantage to ABC of installing solar panels in its factories. *[6 marks]*

....

....

....

....

....

....

....

....

d Do you think ABC should respond to environmental issues by reducing the waste produced during manufacturing? Justify your answer. *[8 marks]*

....

....

....

....

....

....

....

....

....

....

31 Business and ethical issues, and pressure groups

More and more consumers across several different countries are becoming concerned about the ways businesses operate. Pressure groups have criticised the directors of ABC for not making ethical decisions when producing motorbikes and for trying to keep costs low.

Suppliers of motorbike components in some countries are not always paid a fair price for their products and some of ABC's competitors have employed children in their factories in some countries, where wages are low.

There are several competitors of ABC that also use similar practices when manufacturing their products. Pressure groups have tried to organise a boycott to force motorbike manufacturers to change their ways.

1 a What is meant by 'making ethical decisions'? [2 marks]

....

....

....

b Outline **two** examples of ethical business issues for ABC. [4 marks]

....

....

....

....

....

....

c Explain **one** advantage and **one** disadvantage to ABC of responding to ethical issues. [6 marks]

....

....

....

....

....

....

....

....

6 EXTERNAL INFLUENCES ON BUSINESS ACTIVITY

d Explain **two** ways pressure groups could influence the business decisions made by ABC. Which way is likely to have the most effect? Justify your answer. *[8 marks]*

External influences on business activity: end-of-section case study

Use all the information at the start of the questions for Chapters 28, 29, 30 and 31 to help you answer the following questions.

1 a Explain **four** ways ABC can become more environmentally friendly. [8 marks]
  b Consider the effects on ABC of the following economic changes in Country X. Which do you think will have the biggest effect on ABC? Justify your answer. [12 marks]
    i   Falling unemployment.
    ii Falling interest rates.
    iii Depreciation in the exchange rate of Country X.

a ....

b ....

6 EXTERNAL INFLUENCES ON BUSINESS ACTIVITY

....
....
....
....
....
....
....
....
....
....
....
....
....

2 a Explain **two** likely effects on ABC if it does not act in an ethical way. [8 marks]
  b Consider the following **two** options that ABC could take before selling into global markets. Which option should ABC choose? Justify your answer. [12 marks]
    i Set up its own factories to manufacture its products in the main markets in other countries.
    ii Produce new, different styles of motorbikes for the main markets in other countries but keep production in Country X.

a ....
....
....
....
....
....
....
....
....
....

b

Reinforce learning and deepen understanding of the key concepts covered in the latest Cambridge IGCSE™, IGCSE (9-1) and O Level Business syllabuses (0264/0774/7081) with this updated Workbook. An ideal course companion or homework book for use throughout the course.

» Develop and strengthen skills and knowledge with a wealth of additional exercises that perfectly supplement the updated Sixth Edition Student's Book.

» Build confidence with extra practice for each lesson to ensure that a topic is thoroughly understood before moving on.

» Fully explore and analyse international businesses through exercises based on authentic and up-to-date global case studies.

» Keep track of students' work with ready-to-go write-in exercises.

» Save time with all answers available FREE to download from: hachettelearning.com/answers-and-extras

This text has not been through the endorsement process for the Cambridge Pathway.

Also available:
Cambridge IGCSE and O Level Business Student's Book, Sixth Edition
9781036010645

The Student's Book is endorsed for the Cambridge Pathway.

For over 30 years we have been trusted by Cambridge schools around the world to provide quality support for teaching and learning.
For this reason we are an Endorsement Partner of Cambridge International Education and publish endorsed materials for their syllabuses.

Visit us at hachettelearning.com

ISBN 978-1-0360-1072-0